1 MONTH OF
FREE
READING

at

www.ForgottenBooks.com

By purchasing this book you are eligible for one month membership to ForgottenBooks.com, giving you unlimited access to our entire collection of over 1,000,000 titles via our web site and mobile apps.

To claim your free month visit: www.forgottenbooks.com/free234091

ISBN 978-0-483-69566-5
PIBN 10234091

For support please visit www.forgottenbooks.com

Among the Trees Agai

By Evaleen Stein

The Bowen-Merrill Company
Indianapolis

To the memory of my beloved brother
Orth Harper Stein

CONTENTS

Among the Trees Again

I saw a meadow-land one day;
  The grass stood green and high,
But naught appealed in any way
  To stay the passer-by.

Till suddenly the sunlight strayed
  Those leafy tangles through,
And touched to fire, on every blade
  A golden network grew!

A million airy cobwebs gleamed
  So silken-soft and bright,
That all the level lowland seemed
  A tracery of light.

And as I watched the webs, I thought
  The field of life along,
As slight as these, so I have wrought
  With slender threads of song.

They bind the grass, and blossoms, too,
  The bee and butterfly,
And some go faintly wavering through
  The tender azure sky.

Yet still I wait that golden glow
  Whose fine transmuting art
Must smite my web of song, and so
  Reveal it to the heart.

Ah therefore, thou, I pray thee, touch
  These frail threads I have spun,
With grace of sympathy, for such
  Might light them like the sun!

AMONG THE TREES AGAIN

Aye, throb, my heart! is it not sweet to be,
  To breathe, to bide, by growing things once more!
      We did not guess before
How close our life was locked in greenery.
Hark! how the sparrows in the apple tree
  Are chattering, chirping, till their tiny throats
Are fairly brimmed and quivering through and
      through
          With rollick notes!
      Good morrow, little birds!
Good morrow! morrow!—O, *I* would *I* knew
      Some light-winged language, kindred singing
          words
          Wherein to say
  This day, this day, at last this happy day
I come to be a neighbor unto you!

Too long, too long, we heard strange footsteps pass,
  Harsh, strident echoes stricken out of stone;
But never softened by green, growing grass,
  Or mellowed to faint, earthy undertone.
          And then, O heart,
Did we not ofttimes feel ourselves apart,
          Alone,
  Wrought to vague discord by some touch un-
      known?

Did we not weary with a nameless grief,
  In dreaming of tall clover, daisy sown,
        Or music blown
From the wind-harping of some little leaf?

It was not that within the city's core
  There dwelt no sympathies, nor interests keen,
    No human ties to temper its fatigues.
—'Twas only that we needed something more;
        Some note rang wrong;
A foolish fancy, may be, but still strong,
  That life sang sweeter snatched between the green
    Close-lapping verdure of a fret of twigs.

Where all the ground was paven out of sight,
  And only from a far-off strip of sky
    My mother Nature strove to speak to me,
I could not harken to her voice aright;
        I knew not why,
  But ever to mine ears some whispering tree
Seemed of the inmost golden soul of her,
        The best interpreter.
  And so what wonder, Life, that you and I,
Shut out from such glad confidence, should miss
        And grieve for this.

—But all this yearning we'll forget; for now
        Within my window,
            So,
        By finger-tips,
I'll draw into mine arms this dancing bough,
  And stroke its silky buds across my lips.

O generous-natured, friendly, neighbor tree!
   Weave gentle blessings in the shade and shine;
And granting gracious patience to my plea,
   Some simple lesson of your lore make mine,
         Make mine, *I* pray!
O, be a kindly teacher unto me,
   And I'll pour out such worshipful heart-wine,
Not any bird that sings to you all day,
   Or nestles to low, leafy lullaby,
Shall hold you in such dear observance, nay,
   Nor love you half so tenderly as I.

THE REDBIRD

SWEPT lightly by the south wind
  The elm leaves softly stirred,
And in their pale green clusters
  There straightway bloomed a bird!

His glossy feathers glistened
  With dyes as richly red
As any tulip flaming
  From out the garden bed.

But ah, unlike the tulips,
  In joyous strain, ere long,
This redbird flower unfolded
  A heart of golden song!

THE WISHING-SPRING

I KNELT beside the fairy spring,
  Among the tasseled weeds;
Far off, with dreamy murmuring,
  The wind piped through the reeds.

Once, twice, the brimming cup *I* raised
  With trembling finger-tips,
And in its limpid crystal gazed,
  Nor laid it to my lips.

Ah me! the eager heart-desires,
  So thronging swift they came,
My spirit surged like wind-swept fires,
  I knew not which to name.

—Then all at once, *I* quickly quaffed
  The shining drops; but lo,
The wish with that enchanted draught
  No man must ever know!

APRIL MORNING

I LEAN upon the bridge's rail,
　In idle joy, and gazing down,
So watch the frothy bubbles sail,
And bits of tangled grasses trail
　Along the current's tawny brown.

The river flows at full to-day;
　And though within the tide it pours
　There grow no mocking sycamores,
Nor any crystal hints betray
　The spicewood thickets, nor the pale
Soft willow wands of pearly gray,
　Whose interwoven mazes veil
　　The fretted banks, yet here and there,
　　Adown some swirling eddy, where
　　A delving sunbeam shines,
　　　What mines
Of gleaming, streaming, liquid gold
　　The waters hold!

And so, by rapid currents rolled
　In billowy swells that break and chime
In riotous tumult uncontrolled,
The March flood plashes past the pier;
But through its sweeping tones, *I* hear

The sweet, receding murmurs rhyme
The burden of the April time;
   And throbbing like a glad refrain,
Now far, now full, now far again,
   The freshened breeze
Blows gaily, bringing pure and clear
   The fitful, tinkling cadences.

But listen! faint, from out the sheer
   Deep borders of the morning sky,
   Slips down the distance-softened cry
   Of shy wild geese that northward fly;
It vibrates nearer, and more near,
   —And see!
   There! wheeling into sight,
   Far as the vision may descry,
   A level-winged advancing "V,"
They keep their swift, unswerving flight.
   North, north, beyond that scudding fleece
   Of tiny clouds, like wilder geese,
   That join their ranks, and journey, too,
On,—on,—into the farthest blue.

Then, from the boundless space above,
   I drop my dazzled eyes to view
The soft field-grass and meadow-rue,
The restful, brown earth, that *I* love.
   A trick of blinding sun, maybe,
That halo on the hills may prove—
   And yet, they are so dear to me,
   The golden glory that they wear
   Is like none other anywhere,
And, in my heart, *I* hold it true.

Though, surely, what least loving eye
　　Could wander up the river there,
And see aught otherwise than I?
　　　　Or could deny
　　That yonder little glimpse is fair?
The slender point of jutting land
　　Where, faintly burgeoning anew
With rounds of downy buds, there stand
　　　A score of water-willow trees
　　　In clustered tufts, and twinkling through,
　　Across the stream, beside of these,
A line of shining yellow light;
　　　　And half in sight,
And hidden half, upon the right,
　　By wild red-sumac shrubberies,
A windmill, rising tall and white,
　　Slow turning in the breeze.

And then beyond—but how express,
　　What word in any tongue conveys
The depth of dreamy tenderness
　　That laps, and wraps, and overlays
　　　The far blue hills,
　　And spills and fills
　　The valleys with pale purple haze?
O, what sweet syllables confess
　　The glad heart-happiness that plays
　　Through all my pulses as *I* gaze,
　　And drink the beauty, past all praise—
The old, immortal blessedness
　　　Of April days!

ON HEARING THE BALLAD "ALLEN PERCY"

A PLAINTIVE song, so strangely sweet and old,
That all my soul within itself would fold
    And gently keep so quaint a melody,
That like a bird's its notes of liquid gold
    Might oft repeat their sweetness unto me.

A tale of joyless splendor long ago,
Of wedded lady and of loveless woe,
    How she to soothe her sick heart's misery
Cradled in vines her little child, and so
    Sang of dear love beneath a greenwood tree.

And through it all there runs such saddest plaint,
As sweet as lutes, now murmurous, now faint,
    Till, like the far-heard sighing of the sea,
It sweeps in gathering passion past restraint,
    Then breaks, and croons in mournful minor key.

Ah, well-a-day! *I* listen breathless till
I half believe that sorrowing singer still
    Dreams on divinely by the whispering tree;
For in your voice all tenderest heart-strings thrill,
    And all the woodland's marvelous minstrelsy!

MY LITTLE MASTER

O LITTLE poet, winging through
The sheer, clear blue,
Is it the sky you're singing to?
　　Or is it that afar you see
　　Some leafy, laden apple-tree,
　　And half concealed and half confessed,
　　　　A nest?
Ah, truly now, *I* would *I* knew
　　The happy secret of your glee,
　　That joy wherewith you birds are blest,
　　　　Red-breast!

So airy and so light of wing,
You soar and sing,
I pray, could you not softly fling,
　　My merry minstrel, down to me
　　Some echo of that melody
　　That spills from out your tiny bill?
　　　　Some trill
Of all those liquid tones that ring
　　So full of purest poetry,
　　That rhyme, and chime, and thrill, until
　　　　They fill

These vibrant seas of azure air,
Whose blue tides bear
Their witching sweetness everywhere?
     O little master, heed to me!
     And ah, so true, so tenderly,
  I'll learn to sing how lovely grows
          This rose,
Till, by and by, dear heart, I'll dare
     To touch some bolder note, maybe,
  Some chord whence deeper music flows;
          Who knows?

THE NORTHMEN'S SONG OF THE POLE

The roar of the seas where the freezing clouds lower,
  The shriek of the storm-wind, the turbulent tide,
The conquering currents, all vaunt of their power,
  And taunt with the centuries' secret they hide.

Of towering icebergs and glittering floes,
  The sun of the midnight in luminous rings,
Of hopes held at bay by beleaguering snows,
  Of man in his weakness the fierce ocean sings.

Bright over the sky the aurora is red,
  And crimson as life-blood the snowflakes below;
Swift updarting streamers of fire overspread
  All heaven and earth with a roseate glow

Hark! Hark! to the rumble, the thunderous roar
  Of the ancient ice-mountains that shatter and rend
And crash with the tide dashing up on the shore,
  In turmoil titanic and toil without end.

O, woe to the ship that the pitiless clutch
  Of those crushing ice-demons drags down to her
    doom!
The path to the pole is o'er-scattered with such,
  And deep sleep the heroes the tempests entomb.

Beneath the wan moon of the long arctic night
   The frost-smitten sea stretches boundless and lone;
The Shores of the Dead Men loom spectral and
     white,
   In Helheim, the death-goddess waits for her own.

But ho, to her hatred! the soul of the brave
   He bears not who dares not her fury defy!
And ho, to her giants of wind and of wave!
   We crave but to meet and defeat them, or die!

Farewell, and farewell!—the anchor rope strains,
   Loose cable and canvas, and hasten we forth!
The fire of desire quivers hot in our veins,
   We must sail with the gale, to the north! to the
     north!

Must speed with the blast to its ultimate goal,
   The path of its pinions must follow and find
The lure of the ages, the boreal pole,
   And the measureless halls of the house of the
     wind!

IN THE MISSION GARDEN, SAN GABRIEL

O GOLDEN day, wherein at last,
Long leagues and wintry overpast,
   I stand beneath a sky as blue
   As April violets drenched in dew,
   And live within a dream come true!

From rosy-berried pepper-trees
The winds blow spicy fragrances;
   The palms sway softly to and fro,
      And down below,
Between the glossy leaves of these,
   The sparkling, yellow sunbeams steep
The mission garden, where the bees
      Are hoarding deep
Of heliotrope that hangs the wall
As for some princely festival,
      While white and tall
Bright lilies bloom in grace untold,
   And those rare roses, passing all
In splendor, called "The Cloth of Gold!"

O heart, my heart, throb high and fast
   With rapture! for how couldst thou know
   Amid the far-off frost and snow

Where all the skies are overcast
  And shrill and chill the north-winds blow,
    How couldst thou know
December heavens anywhere
    Could show such rare
Such tender and divinest guise,
    That earth and air
Could weave such strange, resistless spell
As this that folds us flower-wise
    At sweet San Gabriel!

San Gabriel! the holy words
  Fall soft as music on the ear;
  I think they are as sweet to hear
As any song of summer birds;
    And harkening them, the while in clear,
      Pure, quivering notes,
  The ancient bells begin to chime,
In shadowy-wise before me floats
  A vision of the vanished time.
    I see again
The little band from sunny Spain,
Those godly ones, and full of grace,
    And without stain,
  Who, heeding neither toil nor pain,
Desiring men of every race,
That such might see sweet Jesus' face,
  And that at length the Lord might reign
    Among all peoples, even so,
Sought in the wilderness this place,
  And consecrated, long ago.

And gazing on the sacred pile
  Their hands upreared in loving zeal,
My heart goes forth to them the while,
  Those faithful fathers, true and leal!
How oft along each cloistered aisle
  They counted o'er and o'er their beads,
While in this garden, unawares,
  The fragrant flowers sowed their seeds.
—And richly as the flowers, the prayers
  Bore fruit in gentle deeds!

In arched embrasures, lifted high
      Against the sky,
The bells in clear-cut beauty show;
  And loftier still, surmounting all,
  And blessing thus the ancient wall,
A cross,—and on its summit, lo!
  A slender bird with pearly breast
    Sits peacefully at rest!

Ah me! Ah me! I know not why
  This little bird with folded wings,
The cross, the tender azure sky,
  Their pure, exceeding beauty brings
Swift tears, and smites my heart, till I
      Am almost fain
  To hide mine eyes for very pain!

Yet though thus for a little space
      I bow my face,
      Nor any grace
  Of rose or lily can I see,
  I know the while that memory,

Clear-eyed and free,
Upon my heart is graving deep
Each least, sweet loveliness, to keep
  Through all the coming years for me.
      And it shall be,
In afterwhiles, when far away,
When wintry skies are bleak and gray
      And no birds sing,
  I shall grow glad remembering
The sweetness of this scarlet day.

DREAM ECHOES

A LITTLE while ago I caught,
  In cadence pure and clear,
A waft of faintest music, wrought
  Upon my inner ear.

A part of some elusive theme
  Whose sweetly solemn air
My soul had harkened in a dream,
  I know not when nor where.

I only know my heart-strings stirred
  With strange, forgotten pain,
That crept upon me as I heard
  That unremembered strain.

A sense of loneliness untold,
  So boundless, deep, unknown,
I blindly reached my hands to hold
  Your palms within my own!

APRIL CONTRADICTIONS

I WATCH the little pear buds break
  And slip their silky sheaths,
And flowers on the maples make
  A thousand russet wreaths,
    —Then something blinds my sight, and I
    Am full of grief, yet know not why!

A rosy purple half betrays
  The wealth the lilacs fold;
The torches of the tulips blaze
  In flames of red and gold;
    Peach boughs are blossoming above,
    —But oh, the vague heartache thereof!

The blue sky wears in gentle wise
  Its loveliness again;
All April sunshine,—yet mine eyes
  Are brimmed with April rain!
    The presage of sweet days to be,
    So strange a sadness stirs in me!

A PLEA

Two years ago, it is two years to-day,—
It seems a score!—since that sweet, bloomy May
When on the barren sea you sailed away.
   The peach-trees then were in a rosy glow,
      And down below,
   The tulip buds had just begun to show.
      —And yet, dear heart, I know
Though all the heaven smiled in tender blue,
      It shone not so to you.
Sorrow had hooded all your skies in gray,
And when these dancing boughs put on their gay,
   Bright May-time bravery, they only grieved
      A heart bereaved.
And though glad robins sang to you to stay,
   And by the stream the first sweet-flags unfurled
Seemed nature's truce to sorrow,—every way
Held warring memories wherewith to gainsay
   And send you wandering over half the world.

Ah, well do I remember how my prayers
Went with you, dear, and followed unawares;
   So speeding ever, winging far and wide
   About the path wherein your ship should ride,
And pleading Heaven that most gentle airs
      And tempered tide
Might bear you safely to the farther side.

Then, when I knew your voyage over,—then,
   —For surely now, at last, I may confess,
   Now that I have outgrown its bitterness,
Though, sometimes, I can almost feel again,
   Remembering those days, that keen distress,
   Yes, jealousy it was! not any less,
       That constantly
Wrapped all my thoughts of you beyond the sea!—
   I feared lest other lives, more large and wide
   Than mine has been, might, day by day, divide
And win your life and love away from me.
   And I was fearful for dear nature, too;
       I could not bear
To think that heaven anywhere should wear
   A hue more deeply, more divinely blue
   Than this home sky that we together knew;
       Or that there grew
Strange bud or bloom to make the earth more fair.
   —A most unworthy fancy, it is true;
Since nature is but nature everywhere,
   The same kind mother, in whatever land;
   So too, maybe, could we but understand,
All hearts and loves are only as a part
       Of one great Heart
   Whose universal pulses so expand
That any lesser life that therein beats
   Should no more dream of this word "jealousy"
   Than yonder shining flakes of bloom should be
Jealous, forsooth, of the whole hawthorn tree
That is but one with their own mass of sweets.

And so, at last, through blind, unreasoning grief
      Beyond belief,
  Brightly within my heart there did uprise
  Love's loyalty, rebuking in this wise:
"Has she not spoken, oft and oft again,
  These three plain words 'I love you'? Wherefore,
      then,
      What right have you
  To deem mere distance could her love undo?
  To fancy aught exists that could estrange
  Her heart from yours, wherein there is no change,
    Or judge her own to be less simply true?"

And then, in shame, I swiftly put aside
All faintest questioning; thenceforth to abide
In trust as pure, as boundless, and as wide
As still sea-deeps, unvexed of any tide.
    Nay, I have learned to cherish rightly, too,
    All light and life that minister to you.
      I hold most dear
    Whatever least thing brings you smallest cheer;
And, day by day, my ceaseless prayer is this,
    That from the changeful, many-colored grace
      Of time and place,
Your grief may come to weave a chrysalis
    Round its dead hopes, till waking, by and by,
    It shall find wings to bear it to the sky.
—But, dear,—God knows I would not do you
      wrong,
Nor touch one heart-string if it be not strong,—
      But O, so long,
So long it seems! You have been gone so long!
    The feather-grass is growing green and high,

And, piping gaily in an azure throng,
The bluebirds spangle all the air with song;
　　Again aflame the rosy peach boughs burn;
　　—Can not you, too, return?

On slender stems the nodding wind-flowers blow,
　　　　And bloodroots grow
Where high the hedges fling their lacing frets
Along the lanes; while, softly sifting through
　　Tall plumy weeds and silver spider-nets,
The yellow sunbeams filter down below
　　　　Until I know
Not any fair Italian sky is blue
　　As is our earth to-day with violets!
Nor do I think that even that Syrian sun
　　You watched ride high above Damascus' towers,
In purer light or richer splendor glowed
　　　　Than any one
Of these most lovely golden dawns of ours
That wake the birds along the river road.
The green ravines are newly fringed with fern;
　　From out the brake a robin red-breast calls;
　　The stream repeats, at rippling intervals,
　　　　"Can you not now return?"

But what avail in striving to compare
　　Earth's endless beauties, whether east or west!
All lands are lovely, and I am aware
That unto me this little spot seems fair,
　　　　More rare
　　Than all the gathered glories of the rest,
　　　　Because I love it best.

And so, in truth, I feel that chief I plead
       A selfish need;
I too, like nature, long to greet the spring!
  Indeed I think I never have confessed,
       Nor have you guessed
How much of May it is your gift to bring.
  You never knew how wintry was the cloud
  Of haunting sadness, that would ofttimes shroud
My inmost being, and creep up to chill
The warmer currents of my life,—until,
      In knowing you,
I felt a pulse like that sweet, joyous thrill
That breaks the buds when all the skies are blue!
The bitter storms of grief I did not fear
      When you were near.
But sometimes now I have grown half afraid
  That unforgotten frost of pain that used
To wrap my nature will again invade
  The singing streams your April touch had
    loosed.
Spring's subtler spells alone I can not learn,
    —Ah, will you not return?

Yet if it chance that prayed-for peace you sought
Be not at length to full perfection wrought,
    If still in vain
  Time strives with memory,—then, dear, I would
  fain
    Let be as naught
  All I have uttered; and I will refrain
From any whispered wish, or word, or thought,
  That might to you in anywise complain.

However much my eager heart may miss,
  How much for you my very soul may yearn,
I will seek patience, confident in this,
  That some time, surely, Love shall conquer pain,
  And then, dear heart, I know you will return.

SEA-DREAMS

I SAT upon the mossy rocks
  Beside the southern sea,
While overhead the summer clouds
  Were drifting lazily.

I watched their purple shadows trail
  Across the sea and hide
Within the hollows of the waves
  That rode the rising tide.

Sometimes the little flakes of foam
  Dashed up in twinkling spray;
And out along their silver paths
  The ships sailed far away.

As through the sun I followed them
  With straining, eager eyes,
From out the sparkling waves I saw
  A shining vision rise.

It seemed a ghostly castle white,
  With battlement and tower,
That hung on the horizon's verge
  By some unearthly power.

I saw its spectral turrets gleam
  As white as ivory,
And wondered who the wizard king
  That reigned upon the sea.

—But while, with breathless gaze, I watched
  This castle, by and by
It vanished in the underworld
  Beyond the sea and sky!

IDEALS

I would that I could weave a song
  As airy and as light,
As are the roundelays that throng
  Within my heart to-night.

I would that I might set to tune
  The beauty of this hour,
When, like a primrose bud, the moon
  Breaks into golden flower.

And all the happy, lilting notes,
  Beyond divinest words,
That nestle in the downy throats
  Of little sleeping birds,

The breeze-borne scent of mignonette,
  That in the garden grows,
Where, strung like pearls, the dew is wet
  Upon the briar-rose,

These things it is, whose voices I
  Have sought for overlong;
Yet still their cunning tones defy
  The artifice of song.

TO THE "WINGED VICTORY OF SAMOTHRACE"

THOU wonder of the warrior prow,
  Supreme, immortal Victory!
Before thy majesty I bow
  And all my soul flames forth to thee!

Within the shadow of thy wings
  A thousand voices sound for me;
In far, tumultuous murmurings,
  I catch the echo of the sea;
The salty surge that rolls more near,
    Till loud and clear
In mighty thunder tones I hear
    The rush of old Ægean tides,
  The bright, white waves that from the shore
  Sweep seaward with unceasing roar;
    In dawning skies the day-star guides,
Across the surf the seabirds call,
    Whilst white and tall
With swift sails swelling over all,
    The shield-hung warship rides.

And like the heaven-born dreams that soar
  From hero spirits, eagle-wise,
  And urge to deeds of great emprise
    And fly before

The eager, throbbing hearts that know
No goal but victory, even so,
Above the restless breakers' roar,
Upon the high cliff evermore
　　Thou standest with bright wings outspread,
　　In all thy fresh-wrought godlihead,
　　　　Beloved of the conqueror!

And as I gaze I seem to trace
The features of thy fearless face,
The matchless marvel of its grace
　　　　That like a star
Across the seas of Samothrace
　　　　Shone forth afar;
I hear the southern winds intone
　　　　Whilst backward blown
　　Thy trailing garments, fluttering
　　From out the slender girdle, cling
About thy limbs and so confess
Their lines of perfect loveliness;
　　Then suddenly o'er everything
　　Great shouts and martial echoes ring!
I see thee, storm-like, rushing past
Thy hand upon the carven mast,
　　And harken whilst thy proud lips fling
The loud, triumphal trumpet blast!

O glorious image! what if time
　　Hath smitten with ungentle touch
Thy perfect beauty? Still sublime
　　Thou art a conqueror, and still
All men unite to name thee such!
　　Before thee all my pulses thrill,

Old hopes and dreams awake in me;
    O Victory,
  Lead, lead but thou mine eager will,
  I follow fast and far until
Some day my ship shall harbor thee!

AS TO THE SUMMER AIR THE ROSE

As to the summer air the rose
    Pours forth her perfume all the day,
For every careless wind that blows
    To scatter far away,

So gives my heart to thee the rare
    Fine fragrance of its sweetest thought,
And thou art heedless as the air
    Whereto the rose is naught!

A WOOD FANCY

THE mandrakes lift, like little mosques,
　Their domes between the vines,
And butterflies for worshipers
　Are flocking to their shrines.

And from tall, tapering mullein towers
　And minarets of green,
The honey-bee muezzins drone
　To bloodroot buds between,

That pilgrim-wise along the road
　Come trooping to the light,
In pale green caftans closely wound
　And turbans spotless white.

While all the way with budding things
　Is tufted thicker than
The praying mats the Persian weaves
　In streets of Ispahan.

And listen! with a lordly note
　Like joyous burst of drums,
In gorgeous gown of gold and black
　The oriole sultan comes!

THE THRUSH

THE creamy dogwood branches,
   The rosy redbud trees,
The drifts of sweet wild-plum bloom
   O'erhung by honey bees,
The gleaming buckeye blossoms
   The south wind blew apart,
Oh, all the woods awaking,
   They overfilled my heart!

Then clear, from out a thicket,
   There rang that golden note
That flutes from none but only
   The tawny thrush's throat;
So charged with all sweet secrets
   The April has to tell,
I bowed my head and harkened,
   Enchanted by its spell.

Till presently that magic
   Heart-melting melody
Drew all my soul to meet it
   In sudden ecstasy.
My spirit found its pinions
   In blessed bird-like birth,
And knew the joyous passion
   That thrilled through all the earth.

The while the thrush was singing,
  I heard the violets stir,
And through the dreamy woodlands
  The breaking buds confer;
I half divined the glories
  Of all the springs to be,
—When, O, the song was silent!
  The thrush had flown, ah me!

MONTEZUMA

On a lofty mountain summit
  In a tawny, desert land,
Lo, a mighty human profile,
  But not hewn by human hand;
In the living rock forever
  Looming dark, majestic, grand.

O'er its outline, heaven fronting,
  When the dawn's first radiance streams
With its rosy touch, and tender,
  Then this face of granite seems
As a sleeper's unawakened
  From the thrall of peaceful dreams.

But when down the western heavens
  Sinks the setting sun, blood-red,
Then the mountain mists that mantle
  Cover close that quiet head,
As men draw a pall of purple
  Round about their kingly dead.

And the stars, like lighted tapers,
  Flicker forth in golden rows
From the heaven's holy altar,
  Whilst the night-wind as it blows
Seems to chant a solemn requiem
  For the passing soul's repose.

Head of royal Montezuma,
  So the ancient legends tell;
Montezuma, granite shrouded
  By some great enchanter's spell,
Lying lordly by the borders
  Of the land he loved so well.

But in silence unrevealing
  Still that calm face fronts the sky;
Heeding neither tears nor laughter,
  Nor if sun or storm go by;
Keeping still its primal counsel,
  In repose, serene and high.

BETWEEN SEASONS

THE cherry trees are haunted
  By hordes of robber jays,
And warmer winds are fanning
  The poppies to a blaze.

And loosed in fitful flurries,
  The sweet syringas fall,
To lie like little snow-drifts
  Against the garden wall.

Upon the laden lattice,
  In softly rounding shapes,
A wealth of tiny clusters
  Are growing into grapes.

Heigho! a drowsy shimmer
  Enfolds the sunny hours;
And humming-birds are hidden
  In scarlet trumpet-flowers.

The tenderness of springtime
  Is almost overpast;
But O, the gracious summer,
  It comes, it comes at last!

A LITTLE LOVE SONG

My heart was like a sunless, cold,
  Unlovely land of ice and snow,
Wherein no blessed buds unfold,
  Nor singing waters flow.

Then all at once the April skies
  Laughed in your look, and at that hour
My spirit melted, torrent-wise,
  My life broke into flower!

O dearest heart, I had not guessed
  What marvel of immortal seeds
Lay hidden deep within my breast,
  Beneath its barren weeds!

But now I know, but now I know
  The glory of the flower of love,
The joyous splendor of its glow,
  The subtile pain thereof!

JUNE

HIGH overhead,
By summer breezes sped,
From every latest burgeoned bough
  The last, spring petals fall;
    And red, red, red,
    Along the garden bed,
The poppy plants are holding now
  Their crimson carnival.

    Clear, sweet, and strong,
    I hear the robin's song,
And catch the merry caroling
  Of some bold bobolink;
    And phlox flowers throng
    The garden ways along,
While peonies and roses bring
  Their pageantries of pink.

    White, gold, and green,
    The lily spires are seen,
And hollyhocks, in stately rows,
  With tufted buds are set;
    Tall, in between,
    The growing sunflowers lean,
And thick the sweet alyssum shows
  Among the mignonette.

Ho! truant May!
Have you, then, gone astray,
Unwitting that in realms of June
   Return were no avail?
     Ah, well-a-day!
So wings the spring away;
The summer's ever oversoon,
   But June, sweet June, all hail!

A SONG OF THOUGHT

O, THE ships have sails for the swelling gales,
  The falcon flies in the wake of the wind,
In the speed of the steed of the Bedouin breed
The blood leaps high to the hoof-beats' lead,
  As the leagues are left behind.
            But what care I
            For the birds that fly,
      Or all the vessels that sail the sea;
            The blasts that blow
            Till the trees bend low,
      Or the barbs of Araby!

I spring to birth with the dust of earth,
  Yet span the heaven from pole to pole;
Or flashing far as the farthermost star,
I know no barrier, bound nor bar
  To hold from my boldest goal.
            The storm's red spark
            As it cleaves the dark,
      With my viewless wings it can not keep pace;
            More fleet than light
            My measureless flight
      To the starless ends of space!

IN THE MOONLIGHT

THE moonbeams filter softly through
  The leaves upon the linden tree;
And as I sit alone, dear heart,
  My spirit yearns for thee!

Yet in some gracious-wise to-night
  We do not seem far worlds apart;
I reach my empty arms and dream
  I fold thee to my heart.

I close my brimming eyes, and see
  The strange, sweet beauty of thy smile,
And fancy that our palms are met
  In loving clasp the while.

In soft, clear tones, I seem to hear
  The long-hushed voice I loved so well;
—I tremble, lest a breath should break
  This moment's happy spell!

O brother mine, could it be true
  Thine own dear presence hovers near
To comfort with this heavenly peace
  Thy little sister here?

BINDWEED

ALONG the lane I idly pass
  Unheeding where the footpath goes,
And loiter through the ripe wild-grass
    That down the open roadway grows
      In feathery, tall tufts that rise
      In filmy tangles, misty-wise;
    The grass that when the south wind blows,
        Shines out and shows
    Shot through with silver lights and rose,
And tiny gold and violet seeds
    That quiver off each gleaming stem
And powder all the wayside weeds,
    And like a glory cover them.

With eager palms I gently press
    Soft sheaves of it against my lips
In sheer delight; and so caress
    And fondle with light finger-tips,
      And watch its beauty when the bright,
        Clear spears of light
      Pierce through its slender leaves and smite
      Their rose and purple, till my sight
Is dazzled with its loveliness!

In verdant nets along the way
  The tendrils of a wild-grape vine
  Through elder thickets intertwine;
And poising lightly on a spray
  Of fruited bramble stems where shine
  Close clustering berries, red as wine,
A little thistle-bird, still gay
  In April's yellow plumage, clings
  With airy grace, and slowly swings,
      And lifts his wings
  In dainty, drowsy flutterings;
They flicker like bright flakes of gold,
  And fan his body, small and slim,
While lovingly the winds enfold
  And summer's heart broods over him.

The sky is softer than the blue
Of cornflower buds beneath the dew;
      And down below
  Upon the marshy meadow swales
  The bindweed weaves its rosy veils
Where thick the blowing rushes grow
Among the tasseled reeds and rue;
  And up between the mossy rails
It lightly climbs, and clambers through
The growing corn, and barley, too,
  And winds the fallow weeds and trails
Along the creek where cowslips grew.

O lavish stems, that fondly fling
Close clasp about the earth, and cling

In wreaths of fragrant flowering,
  Ev'n as ye do
To that dear soil wherefrom ye spring,
 So does my love cleave thereunto!
 And so my full heart-blossoms bind
 The bright midsummer fields, and find
Sweet fellowships with everything!

THE SUMMER SHOWER

The air is shot with spangling drops,
　But heedless of the rain
The sun laughs, through a silver veil,
　Upon the golden grain.

And lightly arching up the east
　In faintly penciled lines,
That throb and flush to tinted bars,
　A double rainbow shines.

It seems to touch the fragrant earth,
　Till, tangled in the breeze,
It winds a film of irised light
　About the distant trees.

In frothy clusters down the road
　The blooming elders lean,
With dripping buds that shine like pearls
　Within a sea of green.

And heaped around them, pink as shells,
　The roses are in flower,
While earth and sky are freshly keyed
　To sweetness by the shower.

AT NIGHT

Come, draw more near! Clasp hands with me!
  Ah close, and closer still!
The night spreads to infinity!
  And through my heart a sudden chill,
    —I pray loose not your loving hold!—
    A fear, a loneliness untold
  Smites sharply, till mine eyes o'erfill!
  Nor have I strength nor stress of will
To set my spirit free.

The cold, the darkness, and the dread
  Immensity of space,
  The great, wan moon, whose ghostly face
For ages has been dead,
The weird lights wheeling overhead,
  The unknown worlds that onward roll,
In endless wanderings ever led,
  That find no goal,
The spectral mists that overspread
  With pallid light the lesser stars,
The lurid glow that glimmers red
  Across the front of Mars,
—O dearest heart, when all is said,
I am afraid! and from the whole
  Wide waste of worlds I hide my sight,
  And from the boundless night!

The ancient mystery of the skies,
   Their silent depths from pole to pole,
The void, the vastness terrifies!
—O, let me rather search your eyes,
    And with your sweet, warm touch disperse
    This terror of the universe
  That strikes into my soul!

THE HOME FIELDS

THE fields are full of sunlight,
  And leafy golden-green,
And misty purple shadows
  Are flitting in between;
The flaky elder flowers
  Are drenched with honey-dew,
And all the distant woodlands
  Stand veiled in tender blue.

Half seen between green thickets
  Of grape-vine and wild rose,
In twinkling swirls of silver
  The lazy river flows;
While down the grassy roadside
  The milkweed balls are bright,
And waving prince's-feather
  Is tipped with snowy white.

Ah, ever-dearest home-land,
  'Tis here my spirit sings!
And as my heart caresses
  The sweet, familiar things,
Such rare midsummer magic
  Distills through all the air,
I think these fields are fairer
  Than any anywhere!

SYMPATHY

To-night a little child lies dead;
 I never saw its face;
I try to fancy now instead
 Its lines of baby grace.

And for the sake of her who weeps
 These lonely watches through
So wakefully my spirit keeps
 A weary vigil, too.

A thousand thoughts appeal to me
 In close-besieging crowd;
But through them all I only see
 A little, snow-white shroud.

Nor may I set dull grief at naught,
 However I am fain;
Since when the heart-strings are dis-
 traught,
 The will must strive in vain.

Ah me! there breaks the dawning sun,
 In golden light serene;
Yet still I mourn this little one,
 Whom I have never seen!

IN SUMMER DEEPS

THROUGH sunny spaces overhead
A gray hawk's lazy pinions spread,
And poppies open wide and red
    Where golden harvests grew.

In rosy wreaths upon the swales
And fallow fields the bindweed trails,
And late-sown buckwheat swiftly pales
    To blossoming anew.

The pond within the pasture land
Reflects the cattle as they stand
In depths of dipping sedges and
    Of tangled meadow-rue.

In silver splashes through the green,
Fine, filmy spider-webs are seen,
And crumpled cockle-flowers between
    Are rifts of tender blue.

On stately stalks of standing corn
A wealth of cresting plumes are borne,
And tawny tasseled tufts adorn
    The ripened barley, too.

So, steeping nature far and wide,
Deep sweeps the flood of summer-tide,
Till all things that therein abide
    Are richly tinctured through.

SONG

O, FRESH from off the ocean
  The salt wind riots through
The fragrant fern and bay-leaves
  And dripping honey-dew.

The morning's on the moorland,
  And flashing, far away,
I glimpse the foam-white seagulls
  And feathers of the spray.

O hasten! let us hasten!
  The tide sings up the sand
The song my heart has harkened
  Across long leagues of land.

So far, far have I journeyed,
  Such weary ways, O sea!
Breathe, breathe me breath of life now,
  And steep the soul of me!

IMPATIENT

Some day, when summer's overpast,
  And loosed by frost, in gold and brown
  These greenly clinging leaves drift down,
    When shrill winds hush
  The robin red-breast and the thrush,
When all the skies are overcast
  With racks of rain, so chill and gray
  Not any burgeoning may be,—
    Some day,
Across far foreign lands and vast
  Unbounded spaces of the sea,
So homeward, homeward, journeying fast,
    At last
  She will come back to me!

I reckon up, in daily sum,
  The time until that scarlet date;
I think the fall will never come,
    So wearily I wait!
  The hours seem leaguing to belate
The days, that never crept so slow;
    And yet,
I used to love the summer so!
  But now my heart may only fret
    And pray for it to go.

And yearning so, with lashes wet,
    I half forget
The greenery on every bough,
  How red the poppies are, and how
 Amid the tufted mignonette
The scented south-winds gently blow;
I heed them not,—I only know
    Time never seemed so long as now!

I search the azure skies in vain,
    No hint of autumn rain!
No hint of fall from bluebirds, nor
Green fields of growing grain.
  Then idly reckoning, as before,
    I strive anew to make less far
    That glad date on the calendar;
    To number less the days that are,
    The changes fixed for sun and star,
The moons that yet must wax and wane;
    Thus evermore
  With fresh impatience, o'er and o'er,
I count the hours;—yet still am fain
To tell them over once again.

O hasten, hasten, autumn days!
  Sear swift this dewy, summer green!
I am grown weary with delays;
    Speed! Speed!
  Bring bitter winds and chill, nor heed
The mellow sweets between!

What if the dead leaves strew the ways,
  And southward all the songs take wing?
    Despite all cheerless frosts that be,
  My eager heart awaits the spring,
  So knowing she will surely bring
    The birds and May to me.

RAIN ON THE RIVER

THE skies are gray, where far and wide,
  Beyond the water-willows,
The marshes spread their emerald tide
  Of blossom-crested billows.

And on the vague horizon's rim,
  In vaporous purple masses,
The distant woods show soft and dim
  Across the lush, green grasses.

An east wind stirs the ivory balls
  Upon the button-bushes;
And hark! a hidden rain-bird calls
  From out the blowing rushes.

Within the water, yonder spray
  Of rosy mallow flowers
Turns faint and pale, till not more gray
  The cloudy heaven lowers.

And all the birches' tender green
  An ashen hue is growing;
While mottled with a silver sheen
  The ruffled waves are flowing.

Then softly through the forest leaves,
    That turn, and toss, and quiver,
The rain, with murmurous cadence, weaves
    A roundel in the river.

It dots the waves with dancing pearls,
    It gleams, and streams, and twinkles;
It sweeps and sinks in silvery swirls,
    And rings, and sings, and tinkles.

The clustering sedges dip and sway,
    Till, after fitful failing,
The sun bursts gaily through the gray,
    And craggy clouds are sailing

Where, southward, in a brilliant sky,
    As light as any feather,
The little moon curves white and high,
    In token of fair weather.

OVER THE SIERRA

FROM out the depths of the abyss,
  Faint echoes of a torrent's roar
  O'er crags whence lordly eagles soar
To poise above the precipice.

A dizzy pathway, sheer and steep;
  A startled catching of the breath;
  And, bearing menaces of death,
A loosened snow-drift's sudden sweep!

Then, blown from out the upper sky,
  Keen, fitful gusts of icy air,
  So light, so tenuous and rare,
The heart leaps strangely swift thereby.

The white moon floating in the calm
  Still ether space, so near, it seems,
  To grasp his eager childhood dreams,
One need but thither reach his palm.

A sense of majesties and mights,
  An exaltation born of these;
  —The summit's awful silences;
A glimpse of Godhead from the heights!

ON THE PRAIRIE

Across the dewy prairie
  The morning wind is borne,
Beyond the new-mown hayfields,
  And through the tasseled corn.

Upon the silver-maples
  It lifts the swinging leaves,
And steals a subtile sweetness
  From rows of golden sheaves.

Within the sunny orchard
  The harvest apples fall,
While from the tossing branches
  The saucy jay-birds call.

In crinkled, fringy clusters
  The scarlet poppies burn,
Where, softly opening, eastward
  The yellow sunflowers turn.

And nibbling in the garden,
  Between the cherry trees,
I see a robber rabbit
  Among the pink sweet-peas.

While with a fitful fanning,
  The lazy wind-mill swings,
About the bloomy peaches
  A robin redbreast sings.

And in the far horizon
  There dwells such tender hue,
These azure cornflower blossoms
  Are not so sweet and blue.

BY THE KANKAKEE

BENEATH the forest trees I lie,
And watch the deep blue summer sky,
And count the white cranes floating by
      On level wings;
And in the undergrowth I hear
A bittern softly treading near,
While through the willows, sweet and clear,
      A wood-thrush sings.

And flashing, plashing, close to me,
With murmurous, melting melody,
The swirling, crystal Kankakee
      Flows deep and swift
Through liquid tints and tones untold
Of topaz, turquoise, bronze and gold,
That in its lucent depths unfold
      And drift, and sift,

Till down among the pearly shells
A wealth of changeful color dwells;
And like a string of silver bells
      The ripples ring
Through trailing water-weeds that raise
Their tangled, yellow blossom-sprays
Where in a green and golden maze
      Tall rushes swing.

And far across the glassy tide,
The marshes shimmer, low and wide,
Where birds and bees and wild things hide
         In reedy grass
Whose wavering, evanescent hues
Pale, darken, change, and interfuse,
Till my enchanted senses lose
         All things that pass,

And only feel an exquisite
Glad throb of light and life complete;
While like some subtile essence sweet,
         The wilderness,
The perfumes warm of wave and wood
The silence of the solitude,
All merge and mingle in my mood,
         Till half I guess

The secrets that the winds impart,
And draw so near to nature's heart
I feel her inmost pulses start;
         While happily
I sink upon her fragrant breast,
Like yonder thrush within its nest,
And deep, entrancing sense of rest
         Steals over me.

THE FISHER FOLK

I KNOW a little village
  Where fisher folk abide;
The dark pine woods behind it,
  The southern sea beside.

There rosy pink crape-myrtles
  In every dooryard grow,
And through the glossy live-oaks
  The salt sea breezes blow.

At break of day the fishers
  Sail out to sea to reap
The harvest that they sowed not,
  The harvest of the deep.

Then, when their nets are emptied,
  They set their sails for land,
To heap the shining fishes
  Upon the shining sand.

Where little barefoot children
  Await them, eager-eyed,
And play the while with sea-shells
  Cast upward by the tide.

And all seem so content there,
  From worldly care so free,
I would that I could find it,
  This secret of the sea!

THE CACTUS LAND

Land of strange, unearthly beauty,
   Tawny Desert, over me
Thou hast cast the deep enchantment
   Of some subtile sorcery!

These thine endless barren reaches
   Where no fruitful harvests grow,
Unto some bring nameless heartache;
   But to me thou dost not so!

Here, where all the air seems newly
   From the springs of life distilled,
Every breath is like a beaker
   With rare, sparkling rapture filled!

And my heart exults and glories
   In the strange, compelling power
Of enchanting, changeful color,
   That is thy supremest dower.

Joy to me thine ever cloudless
   Sky of purest turquoise hue,
And thy rosy mountain ranges
   Wrapped in pale, translucent blue.

Beautiful the rainbow ether
   Shifting, shimmering evermore,
In diaphanous, dazzling splendors
   Over all thy boundless floor,

Where the low-boughed silver sage-bush
   Softly tufts the tawny land,
And the tropic Spanish bayonet
   Clusters tall on every hand.

While for leagues and leagues the cactus,
   Child of sun and sand and bare
Rainless regions, lifts its columns
   Through the rare, transparent air.

Wild and splendid in thy freedom,
   Unsubdued as is the sea,
From the first, O lordly Desert,
   Thou hast drawn my heart to thee!

Desolate thou art, and silent,
   Barren both of fruit and flower;
Yet I love thine arid grandeur
   That defies man's utmost power!

THE LAST SURVIVOR FROM THE LIFE-BOAT

BENEATH his pillow, hid away
From careless sight, the nurses say,
  And safe from any stranger's view,
As miser might some treasure rare,
So does he guard, with jealous care,
      A baby's shoe.

And evermore by day and night,
With burning eyeballs fever-bright,
  This wan survivor of the sea
Scans each blank, closing wall in turn,
In dim endeavor to discern
      If sail there be.

And then the weary sigh that slips
Suspiring from those parching lips
  No heart may hear nor bleed therefor!
As, with hot tears that fall like rain,
He soothes a dying baby's pain
      And o'er and o'er

Croons snatches of soft lullabies
To empty arms held cradle-wise.
  —O human heart-break, love and grief!
God pity him in his distress,
Ev'n as the sea was pitiless
      Beyond belief!

God comfort, as with straining breath,
Unheeding either life or death,
   Yet still with faint unwitting smile,
His fingers fondly seek and fold
The little sea-stained shoe, and hold
   And stroke the while.

THE CASCADE RAVINE

FROM off the traveled road that lay
  Between wide fields of wheat and corn,
  An old gate, gray and weather-worn,
Led down a shady woodland way.

One scarce might trace the narrow path,
  So green it was and overgrown
With springtime's seeded aftermath;
  Tall grasses that had never known
The mower's scythe or sickle's scath,
  And rosy mayweed lightly sown
  Where'er the summer winds had blown;
And all their tangled stems the red
Sweet clover blossoms overspread.

Near by, through scented, leafy veils
  Of wreathing vines, and dewy, dense
Green underwood, a brood of quails
Sped swiftly past the ragged rails
  That tilted off a mossy fence;
And over it, on airy wing,
  A robin paused in glad content
  Where budding elder-bushes leant
And brambles clambered flowering.

Then, suddenly, a low, sweet sound
  Rose, faintly quivering on the breeze,
And all that blossom-studded ground
  Seemed charged with murmurous mysteries!
  As if all rarest forest keys
In dreamful chords divinely blent,
Sang forth from some sweet instrument;
  While pulsing through, with rhythmic beat,
In slumberous melodies there went
The soft susurrus of the trees,
  The wind that wandered through the wheat,
And all the changeful strains of these.

And as I listened, marveling
  Where those light, liquid tones might be,
Forgetting all and everything
  Save that enchanting minstrelsy,
I wandered slowly through the wood,
  Till all at once the parted green
Revealed its secret, for I stood
  Upon the verge of a ravine
 Wherein the sunbeams broke between
Tall rustling hemlock boughs, and bright
As burnished silver in the light,
  A tiny stream ran tinkling through,
While hidden somewhere out of sight,
  A little spring made music, too.

The shining water slipped and slipped
Adown the mossy rocks, and dripped
  From off fine fringing ferns, in drops
Of endless threaded pearls that tipped
  The tasseled sedge and alder tops

With flickering light,—and then it sipped
A drowsy draught of sun, and dipped
  Beneath small clustering buds, and hid
  Among lush marigolds, and slid
    Between tall serried ranks of reeds,
And stroked their little leaves and lipped
    The flower-spangled jewel-weeds;
  Then, speeding suddenly amid
Faint shimmering spray, it lightly tripped
Across white pebbly sand, and stripped
  The marsh flowers' gold, and fled, half seen,
  A splash of silver through the green.

And all the while that music sweet
Kept softly murmuring at my feet,
  As down the rocks in ceaseless streams
    The limpid cascades poured, and still
  The slumberous light in yellow beams
    Bathed the green hemlock boughs,—until
    I seemed to lose all waking will,
  And all my soul was lulled to dreams;
Wherethrough there floated, drowsy-wise,
  Bright glints of bird-wings, gracious gleams
Of tender, sunlit summer skies,
    And fleet, sweet visions of the rare
    Deep, shadowy hearts the forests bear.

FOREBODING

THE scarlet briars trailed across
  The grave I journeyed far to see;
Upon the stone, half hid in moss,
  "Prepare for death, and follow me."

The birds flew southward down the sky;
  Upon a golden linden tree
The leaves that fluttered seemed to sigh,
  "Prepare for death, and follow me."

My father's father slept below
  So dreamless deep and silently,
I spelled the message soft and slow,
  "Prepare for death, and follow me."

—Ah me! 'twas years ago the birds
  Fled swift o'er that far golden tree;
And wherefore now come back these words,
  "Prepare for death, and follow me"?

IN LATE SEPTEMBER

AMONG the hardy marigolds
The spicy gillyflower unfolds,
And in the elm a catbird scolds
    With saucy, outspread wings;
To mellow sweets the pippins speed,
The sunflower disks are brown with seed,
And round about them finches feed
    In clinging, yellow rings.

The latest poppy fires are dead,
But bright as blossoms overhead
In shining sheaves of bronze and red,
    The frost-tipped pear leaves show;
While from their branches blackbirds sing
Or break to noisy chattering;
And slender silken cobwebs string
    The tall grass down below.

Along the uplands, faintly seen
Across the fallow fields between,
The winter wheat grows bravely green
    Despite the coming cold;
And studding all the stubbled ground
In tasseled shocks the corn is bound,
The ripened ears heaped close around
    In piles of purest gold.

To smoky wreaths along the ways
The newly kindled brush-heaps blaze,
And filmy veils of purple haze
    Mesh all the amber air;
Among the fleeces of the sheep
The yellow sunbeams softly creep,
And sweet contentment, wide and deep,
    Rests gently everywhere.

SUNNY NOON

THE rose-trees and the barberries
  Are strung with coral beads;
And fitful breezes lightly sift
  The ripened poppy-seeds.

Still, heedless of the nipping frost,
  Along the garden bed
The white and purple gillyflowers
  Their spicy fragrance shed.

And weaving richest tapestries
  Upon the lattice frame,
The woodbine laces in and out
  In gold, and rose, and flame.

Along the wall the grapevines trace
  Their brown and twisted frets,
And all the trailing clematis
  Is hung with soft aigrettes.

Through fringes that the larches wave
  The sky shows fair and blue,
And somewhere, from beneath the eaves,
  I hear the pigeons coo.

The glory of the noonday sun
  Pervades the dreamy air,
And the sweet heart of beauty throbs
  In music everywhere.

THE GOLDEN WEDDING

More sweet than all the buds that blow
Where summer's rarest roses grow,
  More splendid than white lily spires,
  Or shining, scarlet poppy fires,
Love's fragrant flower,—even so,
  The blossom of the heart's desires.

And richer than all fields enfold
Or all earth's burdened branches hold,
  Than any autumn vintage red,
  Or yellow sheaves new harvested,
Love's ripened fruit of mellow gold,
  The sum of life, when all is said.

EARLY NOVEMBER

O THE sweetness of the jangle
Of the sheep-bells, in the tangle
Of the wild witch-hazel bushes and the spreading
red-bud trees!
—Ah, the silence when it ceases!
But the beauty of the fleeces,
And the soft eyes peering at me through the wood-
bine lattices!

And beyond them, and the network
Of the dogwood, and the fretwork
Of the interlacing grapevines, and across the mead-
ow land,
I can see the color showing
Where the winter-wheat is growing,
With the corn encamped about it like a plumed
protecting band.

While among the many-seeded
Tufts of russet weeds, unheeded,
Truant ducks go idly twinkling through the yellow
stubble-field;
Their white feathers like the glosses
Of the shining silver bosses
That adorn the tawny luster of an olden golden
shield.

In long loops from off the hedges,
Trailing downward to the edges
Of the wayside grass and clover-leaves, fine cobweb
    threads are wound;
Fairy clues that lead my eager
Errant fancy to beleaguer
Some concealed, enchanted chamber in the richly
    covered ground.

Till the sun begins the lighting
Of his western fires, that smiting
Through the orchard boughs are splintered into
    spears of ruddy flame;
An irradiating splendor
That transfigures all the slender
Little leafless twigs and branches with a glory with-
    out name!

O, I know the year is going!
Neither reaping-time nor sowing
Will restore the tender beauty of its blossoms that
    are dead;
Yet I cherish all their sweetness
In the ripeness and completeness
Of the gold and crimson fruitage that my heart has
    harvested.

WHEREFORE WINGS?

HEIGHO, sparrow! Reckless of the rain;
  When chill the cheerless wind grows,
Chirping might and main!
    Is it naught, then, when the rose
      Blows again?

Beating, sleeting on your draggled coat!
  Surely, 'tis enough to drown
Any happy note
  Nestling in that downy brown
      *L*ittle throat.

Ah me, sparrow! Had I but your power,
  Think you in the freezing sleet
I would waste an hour?
  —I'd sing my sweetest to a sweet
      Orange flower!

WINTRY TINTS

THE sky is like an opal,
  And the horizon's ring
Is yellow, like a band of gold,
  To hold so rich a thing.

The wheat-fields are as fleecy
  As any cloud that blows,
But tawny tufts of standing corn
  Prick lightly through the snows.

Beside the drift-bound wind-mill
  A pearly shadow plays
In tones of tender violet,
  And vague, elusive grays.

And tinged with quiet olive
  The hedges fine and bare,
Whose thorny masses down the road
  An alien softness wear.

O, subtile chords of color
  Are fingered by the frost!
Though touched and tuned to colder key,
  No grace of earth is lost.

For see! a deep red ruþy
  The opal heaven grows,
And yonder pool of ice is one
  Great golden-hearted rose!

THE PERFECT FRIENDSHIP

THERE is a garden so divinely fair
   That in its magic bound, surpassing sweet,
   The golden buds, so Persian songs repeat,
Spring forth immortal in enchanted air;
But, ah, a close there is, more heavenly rare,
   Where, cherished warm within the heart's retreat,
   Love's whitest lilies burgeon to complete
And fragrant flowering lovely past compare.

O dearest friend, such lilies have I found
   Within my heart, undreamed-of but for thee!
Nor any fabled buds of genie's ground
   Are sweeter in their immortality;
When thou art near, like notes of happy birds,
My thoughts uprise in songs that need no words.

JANUARY THAW

THE brook has broken through its glass,
   And where the snows were drifted
Round tangled blades of last year's grass,
   The yellow sun is sifted.

Uncovered by the melting night
   And warm, deceiving day-time,
The myrtle bed is green and bright
   As in the midst of Maytime!

I almost fancy that I hear
   The hum of bees in clover,
And from the maples, glad and clear,
   The first red-robin lover.

A mock spring laughs in mocking skies,
   (O little buds, be wary!)
And masking in sweet April's guise
   The youthful year makes merry.

MORNING ON THE MOUNTAIN

Upon the gray crags, steep and sheer,
  The columbines' gold tassels swing,
    And wind-flowers cling,
Where, lightly poised, the mountain deer
Drink in the dewy atmosphere
  In long, deep draughts of sun and spring;
From haunts that know no hunter's snare
  The hermit-thrush and wood-dove wing,
Whilst through green openings squirrels fare
    And here and there
  Great, silvery moths go fluttering.

Along the valley, in a trail
Of purple light, the mist clouds sail,
    And, soft and pale
  As wreaths of newly risen smoke,
They wrap the red-wood trees and veil
  The topmost crests of pine and oak,
And balsam boughs and juniper
Wherethrough the west winds faintly stir
  The underwood, and gently stroke
The tall young ferns, and smooth the fur
  Of countless happy forest-folk.

Wild little hearts, that throb unknown
Save to the fondling winds alone,
   Bright eyes, that sparkle free of fear,
   O earth is sweet, and life is dear!
Here in these forests, still your own,
   In primal peace, this many a year
      God keep you here!
Here where across the waking lands
Young willows wave their bloomy wands,
   Whilst up the heights and far away
The pine trees climb in singing bands
   And feathery spruces surge and sway
And clap their cones, like little hands,
      For gladness of the day!

Up, up, they clamber on until
The tenuous air smites keen and chill,
      And far winds blow
From leagues of everlasting snow;
   And then the mountain buds, more bold,
      Their sheaths unfold
And light their golden fires and glow
   With flame unquenched by frost or cold.

Whilst ever o'er them, shimmering high
      Against the sky,
A glittering, crystal radiance streams,
Wherein the mountain floats and gleams
Through frosty fleeces, till it seems
   That some great morning star, instead
   Of earth, hangs trembling overhead,

A dream of all most lovely dreams!
　An airy miracle, overspread
With veils of silvery tissue spun
Of ice and mist and snow and sun.
A dazzle of all lights in one!

I watch it till, tall towering there
　　Through brightening air,
Such special splendor does it wear
　It seems the sun's own citadel,
　　At sight whereof my lips grow dumb
　With joy I find no voice to tell;
　　So stricken silent, as with some
　Deep gladness of o'ermastering spell;
　Nor any song of mine may dare
　　To follow where
The summit's utmost radiant peak,
　Bright as God's chosen cherubim,
Soars through the smiling sky to seek
　And fearless front the face of Him.

THE LITTLE SISTER

ALONG the street a tiny pair
  Of childish figures lately went;
The boy's face wore a fearless air,
  The little sister's sweet content.

He closely clasped her chubby hand,
  And led her through the throng,
      while she
Seemed perfectly to understand
  He would protect her loyally.

And as I watched them pass from sight,
  My heart began to ache, for so
I held my brother's fingers tight
  And toddled down the long ago.

Then all at once, beyond control,
  The tears uprose in blinding rain,
Such hopeless yearning stirred my soul
  To lay my hand in his again!

              L. of C.

THE SEA-GARDENS OF SANTA CATALINA

LIGHTLY let the boat go drifting,
Neither hand nor oar uplifting,
Let no motion fret the ocean, and no sail be now
unfurled;
Stranger than Aladdin's story,
Lo, the dream-surpassing glory
And the marvel unimagined of the limpid under-
world!

Gaze within the magic mirror
Of the water, crystal clearer
Than the gleaming glass enchanted, made by Merlin's
sorcery
And behold the secrets hidden
Through the ages, till unbidden
Sons of men came sailing, sailing down the blue
Pacific sea.

See the pearl-encrusted portals
Of the caverns, wherein mortals
Dare not pierce with earthly vision, dare not fare
with feet profane;
Coral-columned halls with golden
Thrones in emerald deeps withholden,
·Lit with sparkling amber splendor, where the merry
mermen reign.

See the long kelp banners flying
From their gardens underlying
All the rare, transparent surface of this sunny, south-
ern sea;
Grasses, shot with silver spangles,
Wreathed and caught in starry tangles
Of the purple ocean-pansy and the fringed anemone.

And the brilliant sea-weeds scattered
Like a gay mosaic shattered
In a million shining fragments over all the ocean
floor;
While the bright-hued fish go darting
In swift journeys, meeting, parting,
Weaving gold and scarlet patterns through the water
evermore.

Through the light that throbs and quivers
Down the depths, and breaks and shivers
Into splintered flakes of brightness, that so melt and
interfuse
Into all such strangest ranges
Of translucent color changes,
That the eye is thrilled, bewildered, with their rare
enchanting hues.

—Ah, would thus upon the gleaming
Southern sea, in happy dreaming,
We might drift and drift forever! never shoreward
guide the keel!
Azure skies, forever smiling,
Into visions sweet beguiling,
And beneath our boat the splendor of those rosy
dreams made real!

Lightning Source UK Ltd.
Milton Keynes UK
UKHW012023021218
333216UK00014B/2285/P